CREAT~~IVE TOU~~CHES™  **W9-DDJ-249**

Swags ETC.

THE HOME DECORAT

Copyright© 1996 Cy DeCosse Incorporated 5900 Green Oak Drive Minnetonka, Minnesota 55343
1-800-328-3895 All rights reserved Printed in U.S.A.

Library of Congress Cataloging-in-Publication Data Swags etc. p. cm. — (Creative touches)
Includes index. ISBN 0-86573-876-9 (softcover) 1. Drapery. 2. Drapery in interior decoration. 3. Textile fabrics in interior decoration.
I. Cy DeCosse Incorporated. II. Series. TT390.S93 1996 746.9'4 — dc20 96-26996

CONTENTS

Getting Started

Selecting & Installing
Hardware
8

Installing Mounting Boards
11

Measuring
14

Cutting & Seaming Fabric
16

Easy Swags

Easy Swags
21

Scarf Swags
27

Swag Variations
36

Shirred Swags
39

Nontraditional Swags

Butterfly Swags
47

Rod-pocket Swags
51

More Ideas for
Rod-pocket Swags
56

Buttoned Swags
58

Swags ETC.

One of the most popular window treatments in the world of decorating is the swag. With its dramatic curves and free-flowing form, a swag has the ability to instantly soften the square corners of a window and bring coziness into the room. Swags can be used alone or layered over existing blinds, curtains, or shades for a classy finishing touch.

With the endless variety of swag styles available, there is sure to be a style to suit any decorating scheme. Swag styles vary from structured to relaxed, formal to casual, often with unique features, such as straps or buttons. They may cap the window like a valance, extend partway down the side of the window, or even spill into puddles on the floor. Fabric selection, decorative hardware, and additional trims also help determine the decorative style of the swag.

Though some swags appear to be merely a length of fabric draped over a pole, there are usually hidden sewing and installation tricks used to create that look. Now you can discover the professional secrets of making swags. Clear instructions and step-by-step photographs guide you from fabric selection to final installation, making every project successful.

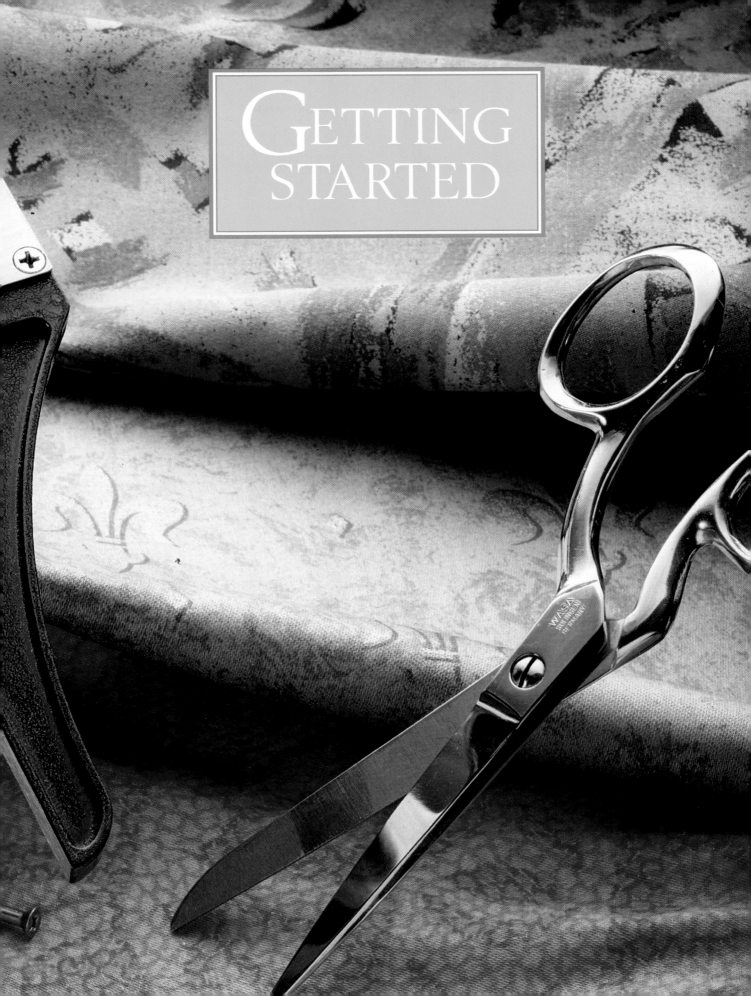

GETTING STARTED

Selecting & Installing Hardware

A

B

C

D

E

F

Careful selection of the hardware is essential to the success of a window treatment project. Decorator rods, pole sets, and decorative accessories enhance window treatments and are available in a variety of colors, finishes, and styles.

Window treatment hardware is packaged complete with mounting brackets, screws or nails, and installation instructions. Use screws alone if installing through drywall or plaster directly into wall studs. When brackets are positioned between walls studs, support the screws for a lightweight treatment with plastic anchors in the correct size for the screws. If the brackets must support a heavy window treament, use plastic toggle anchors in the correct size for the wallboard depth, or use molly bolts. If nails are supplied with the hardware you purchase, use them only for lightweight treatments installed directly to the window frame. Otherwise, substitute screws or molly bolts that fit through the holes in the brackets.

Curtain rods, available in several widths, are used for simple rod-pocket curtains and valances. Select A. CLEAR OR TRANSLUCENT CURTAIN RODS for lace or sheer curtains, to prevent the rod from showing through and detracting from the fabric. B. WIDE RODS, available in both 2½" (6.5 cm) and 4½" (11.5 cm) widths, add interest to rod-pocket window treatments.

C. DOUBLE CURTAIN RODS consist of two rods with different projections mounted on the same bracket. When curtains and valances are used on a window, the inner rod is used for the curtain and the outer rod for the valance.

Pole sets, including D. CONTEMPORARY METAL, E. TRADITIONAL BRASS, and F. WOOD SETS, are available in several styles and finishes. Unfinished wood pole sets can be painted or stained, using any decorative technique.

Decorative accessories, including A. TIE-BACK HOLDERS, B. SWAG HOLDERS, and C. HOLDBACKS, can be used to hold swags in place.

How to install hardware using plastic anchors

1. Mark the screw locations on the wall. Drill holes for the plastic anchors, using a drill bit slightly smaller than the diameter of the plastic anchor. Tap the plastic anchors into the drilled holes, using a hammer.

2. Insert the screw through the hole in the hardware and into installed plastic anchor. Tighten the screw securely; the anchor expands in drywall, preventing it from pulling out of the wall.

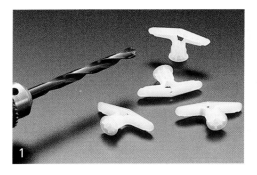

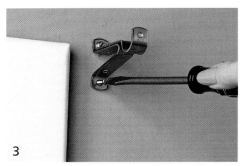

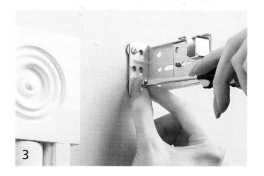

How to install hardware using plastic toggle anchors

1. Mark screw locations on wall. Drill holes for plastic toggle anchors, using drill bit slightly smaller than diameter of toggle anchor shank.

2. Squeeze the wings of the toggle anchor flat, and push toggle anchor into hole; tap in with hammer until it is flush with wall.

3. Insert the screw through hole in hardware and into installed anchor; tighten screw. Wings spread out and flatten against back side of drywall.

How to install hardware using molly bolts

1. Mark screw locations on wall. Drill holes for molly bolts, using drill bit slightly smaller than diameter of the molly bolt.

2. Tap the molly bolt into the drilled hole, using hammer; tighten screw. Molly bolt expands and flattens against the back side of drywall.

3. Remove screw from molly bolt; insert the screw through hole in hardware and into installed molly bolt. Screw hardware securely in place.

Installing Mounting Boards

Many window treatments are mounted on boards rather than on drapery hardware. The mounting board is covered with fabric to match the window treatment or with drapery lining, and the window treatment is then stapled to the board. The mounting board can be installed as an outside mount, securing it directly to the window frame or to the wall above and outside the window frame. Or the board may be installed as an inside mount by securing it inside the window frame.

The size of the mounting board varies, depending on whether the board-mounted window treatment is an inside or outside mount and whether it is being used alone or with an under-treatment. When using stock, or nominal, lumber, keep in mind that the actual measurement differs from the nominal measurement. A 1 × 2 board measures ¾″ × 1 ½″ (2 × 3.8 cm), a 1 × 4 measures ¾″ × 3 ½″ (2 × 9 cm), a 1 × 6 measures ¾″ × 5 ½″ (2 × 14 cm), and a 1 × 8 measures ¾″ × 7 ¼″ (2 × 18.7 cm).

For an inside-mounted window treatment, the depth of the window frame must be at least 1 ½″ (3.8 cm), to accommodate a 1 × 2 mounting board. Cut the mounting board ½″ (1.3 cm) shorter than the inside measurement across the window frame, to ensure that the board will fit inside the frame after it is covered with fabric.

The projection necessary for outside-mounted top treatments depends on the projection of any existing undertreatments. If the undertreatment is stationary, allow at least 2″ (5 cm) of clearance between it and the top treatment; if the undertreatment traverses, allow at least 3″ (7.5 cm) clearance. If there is no undertreatment or if the undertreatment is mounted inside the window frame, use a 1 × 4 board for the top treatment. Cut the mounting board at least 2″ (5 cm) wider than the outside measurement across the window frame. Install the board using angle irons that measure more than one-half the projection of the board.

How to cover the mounting board

CUTTING DIRECTIONS

Cut the fabric to cover the mounting board, with the width of the fabric equal to the distance around the mounting board plus 1″ (2.5 cm) and the length of the fabric equal to the length of the mounting board plus 3″ (7.5 cm).

1. Center board on wrong side of the fabric. Staple one long edge of fabric to board, placing staples about 8″ (20.5 cm) apart; do not staple within 6″ (15 cm) of ends. Wrap the fabric around board. Fold under ⅜″ (1 cm) on long edge; staple to board, placing staples about 6″ (15 cm) apart.

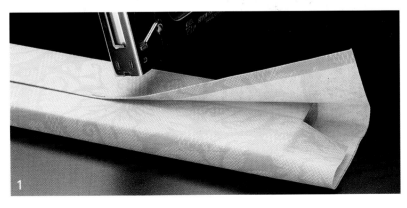

Continued

How to cover the mounting board

2. Miter fabric at corners on side of board with unfolded fabric edge; finger-press. Staple miters in place near raw edge.

3. Miter fabric at corners on side of board with folded fabric edge; finger-press. Fold under excess fabric at ends; staple near fold.

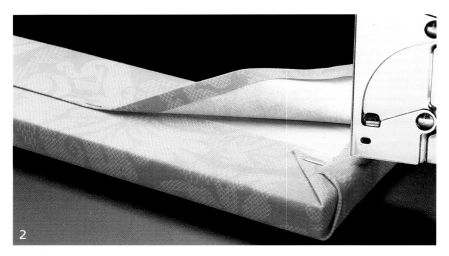

How to install an outside-mounted board

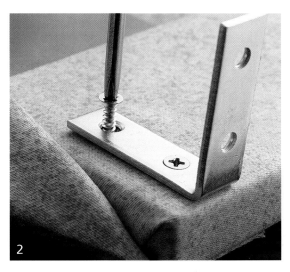

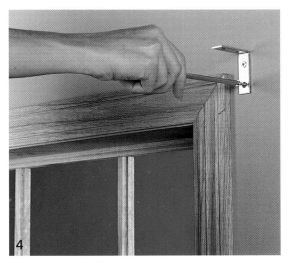

1. Cover mounting board (opposite). Attach window treatment to board. Mark screw holes for angle irons on bottom of board, positioning angle irons within 1" (2.5 cm) of each end of board and at 45" (115 cm) intervals or less; adjust the placement to avoid screw eyes, if any.

2. Predrill screws holes into board; size of drill bit depends on screw size required for angle iron. Screw angle irons to board.

3. Hold board at desired placement, making sure it is level; mark the screw holes on wall or window frame. Remove angle irons from board.

4. Secure angle irons to wall, using 1½" (3.8 cm) flat-heads screws, into wall studs; if angle irons are not positioned at wall studs, use molly bolts or toggle anchors instead of flat-head screws.

5. Reposition window treatment on angle irons, aligning screw holes; fasten screws.

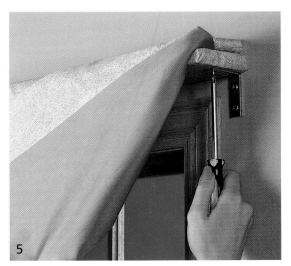

Measuring

Sketch the window treatment to scale on graph paper, to help you determine the most pleasing proportion for the treatment as well as the correct placement of any necessary hardware. After installing the hardware, take all necessary measurements of the window, using a steel tape measure for accuracy, and record the measurements on the sketch.

For each project, you will need to determine the finished length and width of the treatment. The finished length is measured from the top of the mounting board, rod, or heading to where you want the lower edge of the window treatment. The finished width is determined by measuring the length of the rod or mounting board; for treatments with returns, add twice the projection of the rod or mounting board.

Specific instructions for determining the cut lengths and widths of the fabric are given for each project in this book. Yardage requirements can be determined by multiplying the cut length by the number of fabric widths needed to obtain the cut width. When estimating the yardage for patterned fabric, add the length of one pattern repeat for each fabric width needed, to allow for matching the patterns.

TERMS TO KNOW

A. RETURN is the portion of the curtain or top treatment extending from the end of the rod or mounting board to the wall, blocking the side light and view.

B. PROJECTION is the distance the rod or mounting board stands out from the wall. When a wood pole is used, the projection is the distance from the wall to the center of the pole.

C. HEADING is the portion at the top of a rod-pocket curtain that forms a ruffle when the curtain is on the rod. The depth of the heading is the distance from the top of the finished curtain to the top stitching line of the rod pocket.

D. ROD POCKET is the portion of the curtain where the curtain rod is inserted; stitching lines at the top and bottom of the rod pocket keep the rod in place. To determine the depth of the rod pocket, measure around the widest part of the rod or pole; add 1/2" (1.3 cm) ease to this measurement, and divide by two.

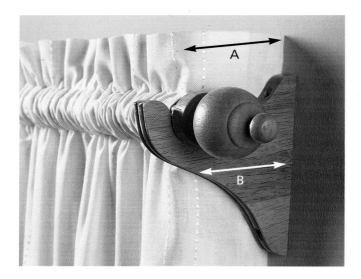

TIPS FOR MEASURING

PLAN the proportion of the layers in a window treatment so the length of the top treatment is about one-fifth the length of the undertreatment. The top treatment may be installed higher than the window, to add visual height to the overall treatment. In some cases, it may be desirable to start the top treatment at the ceiling, provided the top of the window frame is not visible at the lower edge of the top treatment.

PLAN for the shortest point of a top treatment to fall at least 4" to 6" (10 to 15 cm) below the top of the window glass. This prevents you from seeing the window frame as you look upward at the top treatment.

ALLOW ½" (1.3 cm) clearance between the lower edge of the curtain panels and the floor when measuring for floor-length curtains. Allow 1" (2.5 cm) clearance for loosely woven fabrics, because the curtains may stretch slightly after they are hung.

ALLOW 4" to 6" (10 to 15 cm) clearance above baseboard heaters, for safety.

PLAN window treatments to avoid covering heat registers or cold-air returns, for good air circulation.

MEASURE for all curtains in the room to the same height from the floor, for a uniform look. Use the highest window in the room as the standard for measuring the other windows.

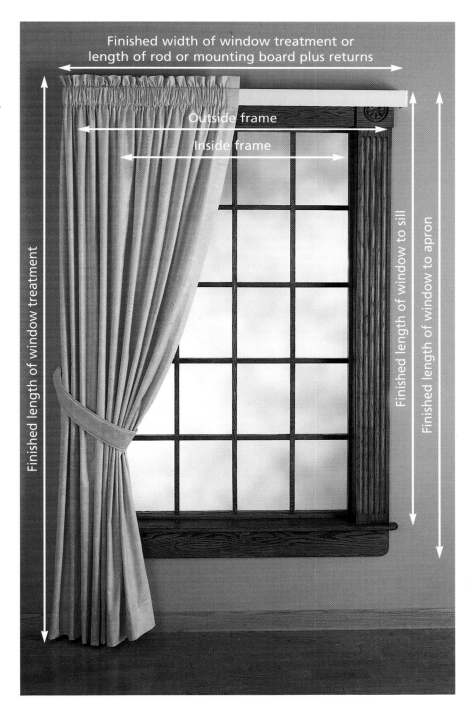

Finished width of window treatment or length of rod or mounting board plus returns

Outside frame

Inside frame

Finished length of window treatment

Finished length of window to sill

Finished length of window to apron

Cutting & Seaming Fabric

When sewing window treatments, a few basic guidelines help ensure good results. The techniques vary somewhat, depending on the type of fabric you are sewing. For any project, it is important to preshrink fabric and lining, using a steam iron, before they are cut.

Many decorator fabrics are tightly woven and may be cut perpendicular to the selvage, using a carpenter's square as a guide for marking the cutting line. However, because lightweight and loosely woven fabrics, such as sheers and casements, tend to slide easily as you cut, it is easier and more accurate to pull a thread along the crosswise grain and cut along the pulled thread.

Patterned decorator fabrics are designed to be matched at the seams (opposite). For window treatments with wide, flat expanses of fabric, it is desirable to eliminate seams by railroading the fabric whenever possible.

Many window treatments look better and are more durable if they are lined. Lining adds body to the treatment as well as protection from sunlight.

TYPES OF SEAMS

A. STRAIGHT-STITCH SEAM, used for lined window treatments, is pressed open.

B. ZIGZAG SEAM, stitched with a narrow zigzag stitch, is used on lace and loosely woven fabrics to prevent puckering; clip the selvages of loosely woven fabrics every 2" (5 cm), allowing the seams to hang smoothly.

C. COMBINATION SEAM, used on tightly woven fabrics, is a straight-stitched seam that is trimmed to 1/4" (6 mm), finished with either an overlock or zigzag stitch, and pressed to one side.

D. FRENCH SEAM is used for sheer fabrics or for window treatments that will be seen from both sides; a narrow seam is first stitched wrong sides together and then stitched again right sides together, encasing the raw edges.

A

B

C

D

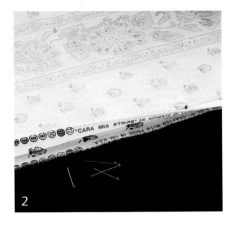

MATCHING PATTERNED FABRICS

1. Position the fabric widths right sides together, matching selvages. Fold back upper selvage until the pattern matches; press foldline.

2. Unfold selvage, and pin the fabric widths together on foldline. Check the match from right side.

3. Repin the fabric so the pins are perpendicular to foldine; stitch on the foldline, using straight stitch.

Easy Swags

Create easy swags with jabots or side panels simply by draping a length of fabric over a decorative pole or decorative hardware. The finished look can range from understated to elegant, casual to dramatic. Swags can be used alone to frame windows, or combined with curtains or blinds to embellish or soften the look.

For an easy, unlined swag without sewing, use the fabric yardage as it comes from the bolt, pressing back the selvages and fusing them in place. The hems of the jabots may be folded either diagonally or straight, then fused in place. Or the jabots can be puddled on the floor without hems, and bishop sleeves may be added, if desired.

Swags may be lined for a finished look on both sides. It is especially desirable to line a swag if you want a contrasting color cascading down the inner edges of the jabots, or for more versatility in draping the fabric around the hardware.

Mediumweight decorator fabric, such as chintz or sateen, is recommended. Avoid heavyweight fabrics, which are bulky to work with and may not drape well. If using a patterned fabric, avoid fabric with a strong one-way design.

The key to beautiful swags is draping and arranging them. For a basic swag, drape the fabric over a decorative rod or hardware, and arrange the jabots as desired. Allow floor-length treatments to puddle on the floor, or plan for the length of the jabots to be about one-third or two-thirds the length of the window. For an asymmetrical look, the jabots may be different lengths, each draped differently.

MATERIALS

- ◆ Decorator fabric.
- ◆ Lining fabric, for lined swag.
- ◆ Decorator pole set, tieback holders, or swag holders.
- ◆ Safety pins or double-stick tape, for securing fabric to pole or rod.
- ◆ Cording, for securing floor-puddled fabric.

CUTTING DIRECTIONS

Use the full width of the fabric. Determine the cut length of the panel by measuring the desired finished length of each jabot and the draped distance between the hardware brackets.

For a lined swag, add ½″ (1.3 cm) seam allowance to this length for each jabot with a straight hem or diagonal hem; or add 18″ to 26″ (46 to 66 cm) for each jabot that will puddle on the floor and 15″ (38 cm) for each bishop-sleeve jabot.

For an unlined swag, add 5″ (12.5 cm) to this length for each jabot with a straight or diagonal hem; or add 18″ to 26″ (46 to 66 cm) for each jabot that will puddle on the floor and 15″ (38 cm) for each bishop-sleeve jabot.

How to make a lined swag

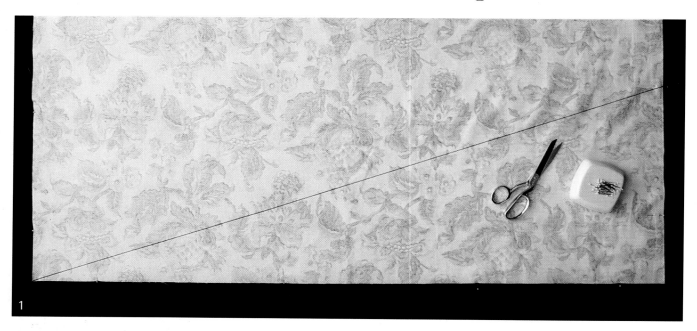

1. Place outer fabric and lining right sides together. If diagonal jabots are desired, pin-mark 18″ (46 cm) from inner corners at both ends of fabric. Draw lines from pin marks diagonally to outer corner of fabric at opposite selvage. Cut on marked lines.

2. Stitch ½″ (1.3 cm) seam around all four sides, leaving 12″ (30.5 cm) opening at center of one long side for turning. Trim corners diagonally. Press seams open. Turn right side out; stitch opening closed. Press edges.

How to make an unlined swag

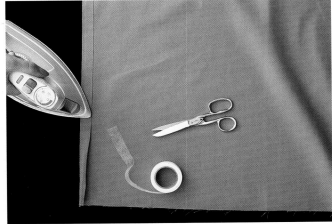

STRAIGHT HEMS. Press in selvages; fuse in place. Fold up 5" (12.5 cm) at lower edge; fuse in place.

FLOOR-PUDDLED JABOTS. Press in selvages; fuse in place. Lower edge of fabric is left as a raw edge, which will be tucked under.

1. DIAGONAL HEMS. Press in selvages; fuse in place, to within 5" (12.5 cm) of outer corner of jabot. At both ends of fabric, pin-mark 5" (12.5 cm) from outer corner of jabot and 23" (58.5 cm) from inner corner. Fold fabric diagonally between pin marks; press.

2. Fold fabric even with fused side hems at outer corners; press. Fuse edges of the jabot in place.

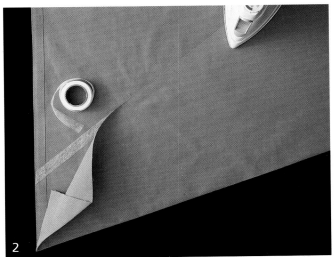

How to drape a swag

1. Drape the fabric over the pole or decorative hardware, placing fabric so jabots are at the desired lengths. If jabots have diagonal hems, the shorter corners of the jabots will be toward the window.

2. Fan-fold fabric into generous pleats at each end where the panel drapes from the pole or hardware. Tug gently on the lower edge of the center swagged portion for desired drape; adjust folds.

3. Adjust folds in jabots. Secure fabric to top of pole or hardware with safety pins or double-stick tape, if necessary.

BISHOP SLEEVES. Install swag holder about 6" (15 cm) higher than desired height for pouf of bishop sleeve. Insert fabric into swag holder. Arrange bishop sleeve, fanning and blousing the fabric. Pin edges of fabric together in the back to keep the hardware from showing.

FLOOR-PUDDLED JABOTS. Gather the lower edge of fabric by hand if the swag is unlined, and tie with cording, tucking raw edges inside; arrange fabric on the floor as desired. If swag is lined, simply arrange fabric in soft folds, tucking under lower edge.

*S*carf Swags

The simplicity of scarf swags makes them a favorite informal top treatment. In this method, the shaping of the swag is achieved by cutting out wedges of excess fullness from a length of fabric at each point where the swag crosses a swag holder. The swag is then constructed by sewing the angled pieces together and adding a lining. Simply fanfold the swag along the seams and drape it over the swag holders, to make hanging the swag virtually foolproof. Make swags that drape into a single swoop or into multiple swoops, adding poufs at the top of the side panels, if desired. This scarf swag uses the full width of the fabric and can be either self-lined or lined in a contrasting fabric.

Swag holders are available in several styles, including medallions and scarf rings; decorative tieback holders and holdbacks may also be used (page 9). Mount the holders in the desired locations at the top of the window before beginning the project, and measure for the treatment, using twill tape.

OPPOSITE: SCARF SWAG WITH POUFS is an easy variation of a basic swag. To make the poufs, simply add extra length to the side panels; then fold and tie the poufs in place.

MATERIALS

- Swag holders; one swag holder is needed at each upper corner of the window for a swag with a single swoop, and one holder is needed for each additional swoop.

- Twill tape.

- Decorator fabric for swag, length determined as on page 29, step 1, for swag with single swoop, or as on page 33, step 1, for swag with multiple swoops.

- Matching or contrasting fabric for lining, length equal to decorator fabric.

SCARF SWAGS can be sewn in many variations. Above, a swag with a single swoop is
held in place with scarf rings.

How to measure for a scarf swag with a single swoop

1. Mount swag holders in desired locations. Drape a length of twill tape over the holders as shown, extending to longest points of tapered sides and stretching straight across top of window. This will be the finished length on the upper edge of the swag.

2. Drape a second length of twill tape over the holders as shown, extending to shortest points of tapered sides and dipping to lowest point desired at center of swoop. This will be the finished length on the lower edge of the swag. Mark both tapes at holders.

3. Measure and record the lengths of the tape for each section. Measurement A is from the long point to the holder, Measurement B is from the short point to the holder, Measurement C is the distance straight across between the holders, and Measurement D is the length of the swoop between the holders.

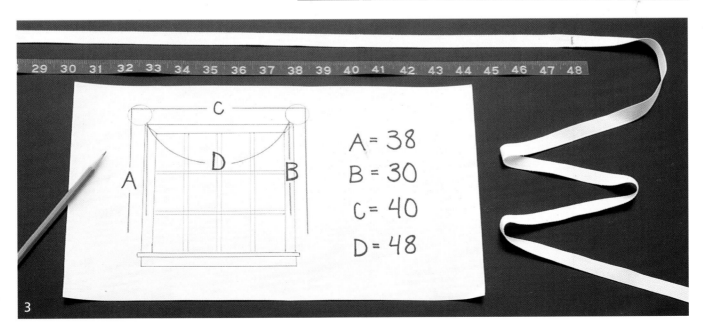

A = 38
B = 30
C = 40
D = 48

How to make a scarf swag with a single swoop

1. Cut the full width of the fabric, with the length equal to Measurement D plus two times Measurement A plus 3″ (7.5 cm) for seam allowances. Measure from each end of the fabric a distance equal to Measurement A plus 1″ (2.5 cm). Cut the fabric perpendicular to the selvage at these points.

2. Turn one end piece completely around, if using fabric with an obvious one-way design, so upward direction on both ends points toward the middle; when hung, the design will face in correct direction on end pieces. Label top of each end piece.

3. Subtract Measurement B from Measurement A. Mark a point on the inside edge of one end piece this distance from the lower cut edge. Draw a line from this point to the lower outside corner; cut away triangular wedge. Repeat for other end piece, cutting angle in opposite direction.

4. Subtract Measurement C from Measurement D; divide this measurement in half. Mark a point on upper edge of the center piece this distance from outer edge. Draw a line from this point to lower corner; cut away triangular wedge. Repeat for opposite side of center piece.

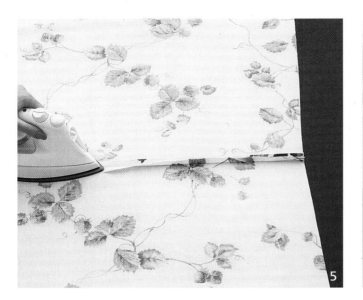

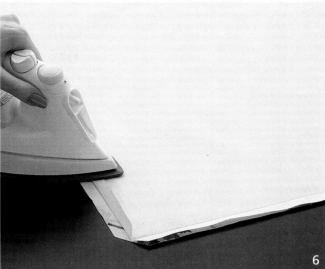

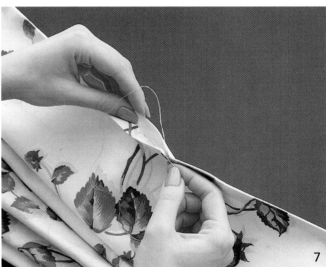

5. Cut lining, using swag pieces as patterns; label tops of the lining pieces. Stitch swag pieces together in ½" (1.3 cm) seams, easing to fit; repeat for the lining pieces. Press the seams open.

6. Pin the lining to the swag, right sides together. Stitch a ½" (1.3 cm) seam around all sides, leaving an opening along upper edge for turning. Trim corners diagonally. Press lining seam allowance toward lining.

7. Turn swag right side out; press seamed edges. Slipstitch opening closed.

8. Fanfold swag along seamlines; tie folds with twill tape. Hang swag through scarf ring or over medallion-style scarf holder or tieback holder. Arrange folds in swag and sides as desired. Remove twill tape.

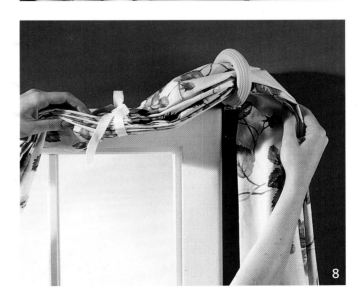

SCARF SWAG with multiple swoops drapes over swag holders mounted at the top of the window.

How to measure for a scarf swag with multiple swoops

1. Mount swag holders in desired locations. Drape a length of twill tape over the holders as shown, extending to longest points of tapered sides, stretching straight across top of window. This will be the finished length on the top of the swag.

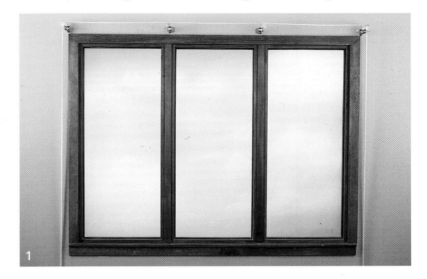

2. Drape a second length of twill tape over the holders, as shown, extending to shortest points of tapered sides, dipping to lowest point desired at center of each swoop. This will be the finished length on the bottom of the swag. Mark both tapes at holders.

3. Measure and record the lengths of the tape for each section. Measurement A is from the long point to the holder, Measurement B is from the short point to the holder, Measurement C is the distance straight across between the holders, and Measurement D is the total length of all the swoops between end holders.

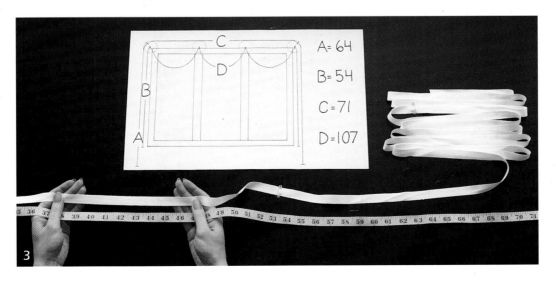

A = 64

B = 54

C = 71

D = 107

How to make a scarf swag with multiple swoops

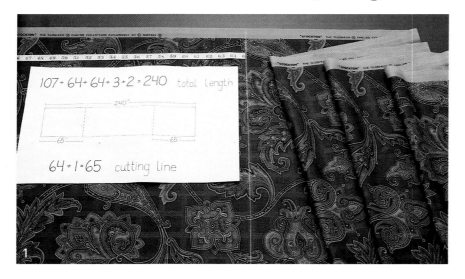

1. Cut the full width of fabric, with length equal to Measurement D plus two times Measurement A plus 1" (2.5 cm) for each swoop plus an additional 2" (5 cm). Measure from each end of the fabric a distance equal to Measurement A plus 1" (2.5 cm). Cut the fabric perpendicular to the selvage at these points. Follow steps 2 and 3 on page 30 for swag with single swoop.

2. Measure the length of the center section; divide this measurement into the number of swoops in the swag. Mark the center section into lengths of this size; cut the fabric perpendicular to selvages at these points.

3. Subtract Measurement C from Measurement D. Divide this measurement by the number of swoops in the swag; then divide this number in half. Mark a point on upper edge of one swoop piece this distance from outer edge. Draw a line from this point to lower corner; cut away triangular wedge. Repeat for opposite side of swoop piece. Cut identical wedges from each remaining swoop piece. Complete swag as on page 31, steps 5 to 8.

How to make a scarf swag with poufs

1. Cut the fabric, following step 1 on page 30 for swag with single swoop or step 1, opposite, for swag with multiple swoops, adding 16" to 20" (40.5 to 51 cm) for each pouf. Measure from each end of fabric a distance equal to Measurement A plus length allowed for one pouf plus 1" (2.5 cm). Cut fabric perpendicular to the selvage at these points. Turn one end panel around as on page 30, step 2, if using fabric with one-way design.

2. Trim wedges from the end pieces, as on page 30, step 3. Then follow steps 4 to 8 on pages 30 and 31 for a swag with a single swoop or steps 2 and 3, opposite, for a swag with multiple swoops; keep folds tied. Tie another piece of twill tape around the fan-folded fabric 16" to 20" (40.5 to 51 cm) below the swag holder. Raise tied fabric to the swag holder bracket; knot securely. Fan out fabric to form pouf. Remove upper twill tape.

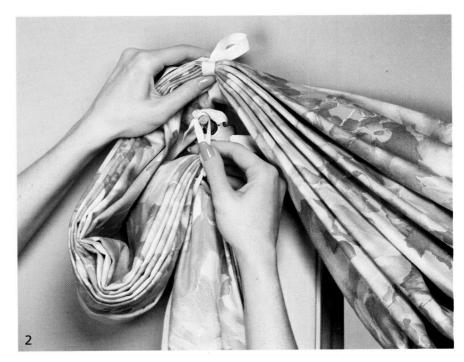

Swag Variations

TOP: SPECIAL DECORATIVE HARDWARE, such as the Swags 'n Tails pole set, is designed especially for swags. On this pole set, the rings hold the swagged fabric in place, and the upper edge of the fabric is held taut to the back of the rod with self-adhesive hook and loop tape.

OPPOSITE CENTER: ORNATE SHELF BRACKETS are used as hardware for this swag, and decorative cording with tassels is draped with the fabric for added detail.

OPPOSITE BOTTOM: KNOTS tied in this lined panel hold the swag on the rod, creating a contemporary look. The fabric has been draped over the center of the rod to create two swags.

ABOVE: BRASS TOWEL RINGS serve as decorative hardware for this swag and coordinate with other brass accessories in the room.

Shirred Swags

Less formal than a traditional swag, this lined, pole-mounted swag is easy to make. Shirring tape, stitched to a straight fabric panel, creates the swag with jabots, or side panels. The jabots on this treatment hang in a loose, unstructured style and are stapled in place to conceal the shirring. Welting, inserted at the edges of the swag, adds a finishing touch.

Mount the swag 2″ to 3″ (5 to 7.5 cm) above the window frame to avoid covering too much of the window. The instructions that follow are for jabots approximately 28″ (71 cm) long at the longest point; this length may vary, depending on the amount of shirring.

For best results, select a fabric with a nondirectional print, so that the lengthwise grain of the fabric can be run horizontally across the width of the window. This allows the swag to be constructed without piecing fabric widths together.

INSERT, OPPOSITE LEFT: TWISTED WELTING is used instead of fabric welting for added textural interest.

INSERT, OPPOSITE RIGHT: SCALLOPED LOOP FRINGE is topstitched to the outer edges of this swag for visual impact.

MATERIALS

- ◆ Decorator fabric.
- ◆ Lining.
- ◆ 2 1/2 yd. (2.3 m) two-cord shirring tape that gathers to at least four times fullness.
- ◆ 5/32" (3.8 mm) purchased welting.
- ◆ Wood pole, finials, and keyhole support brackets.

CUTTING DIRECTIONS

Determine the cut length of the fabric panel by measuring the length of the mounting pole and adding 49" (125 cm) to this measurement for the jabots and seam allowances. Cut the fabric and the lining to this length. Trim the outer fabric and the lining to 44" (112 cm) in width.

How to make a shirred swag

1. Measure the pole length. Center and pin-mark this distance on the upper edge of rectangle cut from outer fabric. Measure the remaining distance around rectangle, from pin mark to pin mark; cut cording for welting to this measurement plus 1" (2.5 cm).

2. Pin welting to right side of outer fabric, matching raw edges and extending ends of welting 1/2" (1.3 cm) beyond pin marks; clip the welting at the corners. Remove the stitching from the welting for 1/2" (1.3 cm) at the ends; remove cording up to pin mark.

3. Stitch welting to the outer fabric, using zipper foot; fold over 1/2" (1.3 cm) of welting fabric at ends.

4. Pin the lining and outer fabric right sides together; stitch around all four sides close to previous stitching, leaving a 12" (30.5 cm) opening at center of upper edge. Trim corners diagonally; turn right side out. Press, folding in seam allowances at center opening. Fold panel in half, aligning upper and lower edges; pin-mark lower edge of panel on lining 4" (10 cm) out from end of welting.

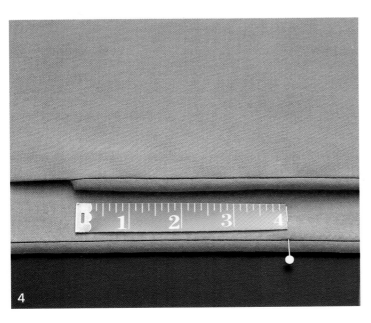

Continued

How to make
a shirred swag
(CONTINUED)

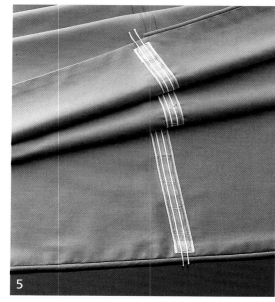

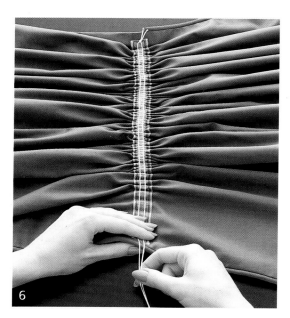

5. Position shirring tape diagonally on lining from end of welting to pin mark on lower edge of panel; turn under 1" (2.5 cm) at ends. Use pin to pull out cords. Stitch tape next to cords, through all layers.

6. Knot cords at upper edge of panel; at lower edge, pull evenly on the cords to shirr fabric. Tie off, leaving long tails.

7. Hold pole firmly against the table; using pencil, draw a line on pole where it touches the table.

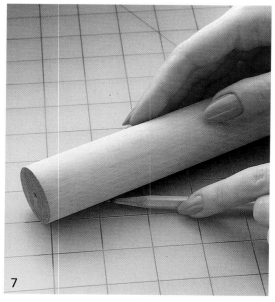

8. Center the swag on pole, aligning upper edge to marked line on pole; staple in place.

9. Pinch jabot fabric 2" to 4" (5 to 10 cm) from upper edge; pull fabric up to pole and staple in place, concealing shirring tape. Secure the finials to pole.

10. Install pole. Adjust length of shirring, if desired; cut off excess cord length.

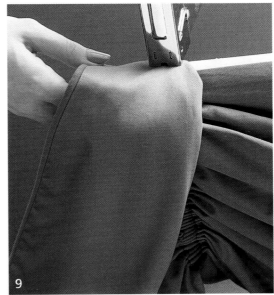

NONTRADITIONAL SWAGS

*B*utterfly *Swags*

Butterfly swags have a simple styling that works well for many decorating schemes. This lined stationary window treatment can be made in any length, from valance length to full length. Its fanfolded fabric is held in place with decorative straps. The folds swag in the center and flare at the sides, creating the butterfly effect.

The swag, attached to a mounting board, may be used alone or over a shade or blinds. If there is no undertreatment, a 1 × 2 mounting board can be used. With an undertreatment, use a mounting board that will project out from the window frame enough so the valance will clear the undertreatment by 2" to 3" (5 to 7.5 cm). The length of the mounting board is equal to the desired finished width of the valance.

The mounting board is installed at the top of the window frame, or just outside it, using angle irons a little shorter than the width of the board. Whenever possible, screw the angle irons into wall studs, using pan-head screws. For a secure installation into drywall or plaster, use molly bolts.

OPPOSITE: BUTTERFLY SWAG can be sewn as a long window treatment for privacy or as a valance to enjoy the view.

MATERIALS

- Decorator fabrics, for swag and straps.
- Lining fabric.
- Mounting board.
- Heavy-duty stapler; staples.
- Angle irons; pan-head screws or molly

CUTTING DIRECTIONS

The cut length of the swag is equal to the desired finished length at the straps plus 25" (63.5 cm); this allows for the pleats, seam allowance, and mounting. To determine the width of the fabric, add the desired width of the swag plus 1" (2.5 cm) for the two seam allowances at the sides plus twice the width, or projection, of the mounting board. Cut the fabric and lining to this length and width, piecing fabric widths together, if necessary.

For straps with a finished width of 1½" (3.8 cm), cut two straps, 4" (10 cm) wide, with the cut length of the straps equal to twice the desired finished length plus 4" (10 cm); this allows for the mounting and the length taken up across the bottom.

How to sew a butterfly swag

1. Seam fabric widths, if necessary. Place the outer fabric and lining right sides together; pin. Stitch ½" (1.3 cm) seam around the sides and lower edge; leave the upper edge unstitched. Clip lower corners. Press the lining seam allowance toward lining. Turn swag right side out, and press.

2. Fold one strap piece in half lengthwise, right sides together; stitch ½" (1.3 cm) seam on the long edge. Press seam open with tip of iron, taking care not to crease the fabric. Turn strap right side out, centering seam on back; press. Repeat for the second strap.

3. Determine desired placement for straps, 6" to 10" (15 to 25.5 cm) from end, depending on width of swag. Pin one end of each strap, right side up, to upper edge of swag at desired placement.

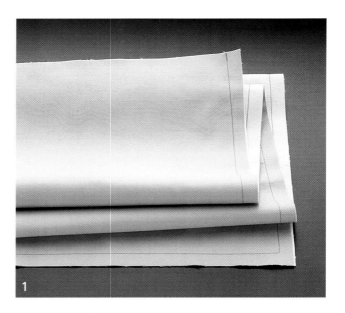

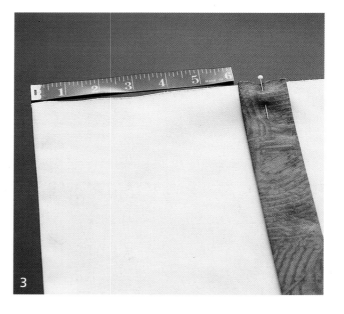

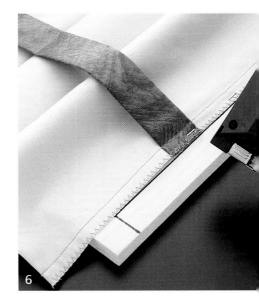

4. Wrap straps under bottom of swag; pin remaining end of each strap in place on lining side of swag, matching raw edges of straps to upper edge of swag.

5. Stitch outer fabric and lining together along the upper edge of swag, securing straps in stitching. Finish raw edges, using zigzag or overlock stitch.

6. Mark lines on top of the mounting board, 1″ (2.5 cm) from front and sides. Center swag on board, with upper edge of the swag along the marked line. Staple in place at 2″ (5 cm) intervals; apply two staples at each strap.

7. Wrap side of swag around end of the mounting board; staple in place on top of board, along marked line, forming a squared corner. Repeat for remaining side. Mount swag as on page 13, steps 1 to 5.

8. Fanfold the lower 24″ (61 cm) of swag. Pull the pleats gently into swagged position at center. Adjust folds as desired near straps.

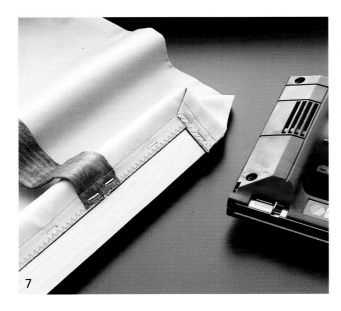

INSTALL the curtain rod or pole. Drape a length of twill tape or ribbon from the rod, simulating the desired shape at the lower edge of the valance. If more than one swag is desired, tie the tape or ribbon into the desired position for each swag. Do not include the width of the ruffle in the depth of the swags. Measuring from the bottom of the rod, measure the length of the twill tape or ribbon.

Rod-pocket Swags

This softly gathered swag valance is a versatile top treatment that can be styled in a variety of ways. For country charm or soft femininity, sew a ruffle to the lower edge. Elegant fabric and bullion fringe (page 57) create a more formal look. The valance can fall in one deep, graceful swag or two swags with equal depths. For yet another look, the valance can be divided to create a triple swag with two equal swags on either side of a third, deeper swag (page 56).

Regardless of the size of the valance or the number of swags, the valance is constructed from a half circle of fabric. Surprisingly, the straight edge of the half circle becomes the lower curved edge of the valance to which the ruffle or fringe is attached. The heading and rod pocket of the valance are sewn along the curve of the half circle. To avoid seams, the length of the straight edge should not exceed twice the width of the decorator fabric.

MATERIALS

- Twill tape or ribbon.
- Decorator fabric for valance; the amount needed is equal to the length of the twill tape or ribbon, as determined at right, plus twice the depth of the heading and rod pocket, plus 1" (2.5 cm). Additional fabric is needed for the optional ruffle.
- Lining; the amount needed is equal to the length of the twill tape or ribbon, as determined at right, plus twice the depth of the heading and rod pocket, plus 1" (2.5 cm).
- Curtain rod or pole set.
- Cord, such as pearl cotton, for gathering.

CUTTING DIRECTIONS

Determine the depth of the heading and rod pocket (page 14). Fold the decorator fabric in half crosswise; trim the selvages. Mark an arc, using a straightedge and pencil, measuring from the outer edge at the fold, a distance equal to one-half the measured length of the lower edge of the valance plus the depth of the heading and rod pocket plus ½" (1.3 cm). Cut on the marked line through both layers. Cut the lining to the same size.

For the ruffle, cut fabric strips on the crosswise grain of the fabric, with the width of the fabric strips equal to twice the desired finished width of the ruffle plus 1" (2.5 cm). Cut as many fabric strips as necessary for a combined length of two to two-and-one-half times the measured length of the twill tape or ribbon (page 50).

How to sew a single rod-pocket swag

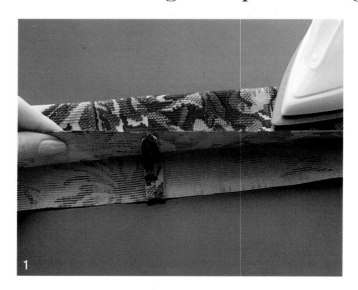

1. Stitch the fabric strips for ruffle together in ¼" (6 mm) seams, right sides together. Press the seams open. Fold ends of strips in half lengthwise, right sides together; stitch across ends in ¼" (6 mm) seams. Turn right side out; press.

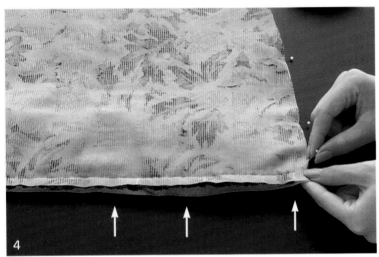

2. Zigzag over a cord within ½" (1.3 cm) seam allowance, stitching through both layers of ruffle strip.

3. Divide ruffle and straight edge of valance into fourths or eighths; pin-mark, placing outer pins of valance ½" (1.3 cm) from the raw edges. Pin ruffle along straight edge of the valance, right sides together, matching raw edges and pin marks; pull the cord, gathering fabric to fit between the pins. Stitch ruffle to valance a scant ½" (1.3 cm) from the raw edges.

4. Mark ½" (1.3 cm) seam allowance and the depths of heading and rod pocket (opposite) on wrong side of valance fabric (arrows), at each end of the straight edge. Pin valance to the lining, right sides together, matching raw edges.

5. Stitch valance to the lining in ½" (1.3 cm) seam, stitching with valance faceup. Leave an opening for the rod pocket at each end of the straight edge, and an opening near the center of the straight edge for turning.

Continued

How to sew a
single rod-pocket swag
(CONTINUED)

6. Press the lining seam allowance toward the lining. Trim the corners diagonally.

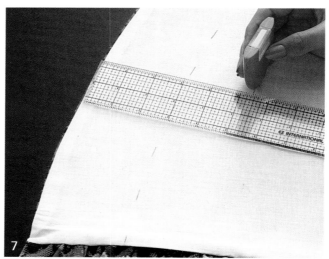

7. Turn valance right side out; press seamed edges. Stitch center opening closed. Mark chalk lines for depth of heading and depth of rod pocket on curved edge of valance. Pin layers together. Stitch on marked lines.

8. Insert the curtain rod or pole into the rod pocket, gathering fabric evenly. Install rod on brackets. Adjust the folds of valance as desired.

How to sew a double rod-pocket swag

1. Follow pages 52 to 54, steps 1 to 7. Place valance facedown on flat surface. Divide the lower straight edge, between the rod pockets at ends, into two equal parts; mark ½" (1.3 cm) above seam. Divide upper curved edge into two equal parts. Holding straightedge at marks, draw a line from lower edge, between marks, to a point 2" (5 cm) below the rod pocket.

2. Cut a length of cord, such as pearl cotton, twice the length of the marked line plus 4" (10 cm). Using zigzag stitch of medium length and narrow width, stitch over cord down left side of line, beginning 2" below rod pocket, to end of line; take care not to catch cord in stitching. Leave needle down in fabric to right of cord; pivot.

3. Continue stitching over the cord on opposite side of the line toward upper edge, taking care not to catch cord in stitching.

4. Secure stitches at top of line by stitching in place over both cords, using wide zigzag stitch.

5. Follow step 8, opposite. Draw up gathering cords to desired height; tie cords. Adjust gathers and folds of the valance.

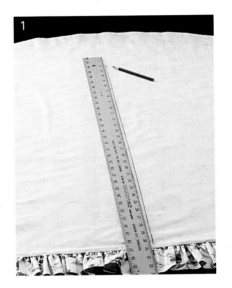

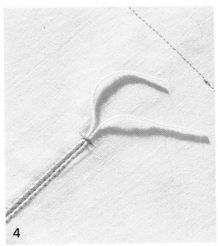

More ideas for rod-pocket swags

LEFT: SINGLE SWAG without a ruffle is sewn with a popped heading. Fabric layers in the heading are pulled apart for a soft, rounded look. The swag is lined with matching fabric.

OPPOSITE: FRINGE-TRIMMED SWAG is made from an elegant jacquard fabric for a formal look.

LEFT: TRIPLE SWAG is trimmed with tassel fringe instead of a ruffle. The swag has a 2" (5 cm) heading and a 3" (7.5 cm) rod pocket. Follow the steps for a double swag on page 55, except divide the lower straight edge between rod pockets into three parts; also pin-mark the upper curved edge about 5" (12.5 cm) from each end, and divide the remaining space into three parts. If window sections are unequal, divide the spaces for swags in proportion to the window sections.

*B*uttoned Swags

Top off a simple window treatment or shower curtain with an easy-to-sew buttoned swag valance, or use the swag over shower doors or blinds. The valance is made up of two parts: a shirred fabric sleeve that covers the rod, and a swag that buttons onto the sleeve.

The swagged fabric has one-and-one-half times fullness. Additional fabric is allowed for the draped fabric at the ends. The number of buttons and the distance between them varies with the width of the treatment. For a 60" (152.5 cm) shower area, it works well to use five buttons, creating just three swoops.

Choose a mediumweight decorator fabric that can support the weight of the buttoned treatment, yet drape nicely between the buttons. Because the swag is self-lined, avoid patterns that will show through the outer layer, especially with window treatments.

The fabric for both the sleeve and the swag can be cut on the crosswise grain, piecing widths of fabric together as necessary. Sometimes, fabric can be cut on the lengthwise grain, or *railroaded*, to eliminate seaming. Railroading can only be used for solid-colored fabrics or patterned fabrics that can be turned sideways; it is inappropriate for fabrics with one-way designs. If you are using the swag with a shower curtain or window treatment, cut both the swag and the curtain on the same grainline.

The curtain rod for the swag should be mounted so the lower edge of the rod is at least 7" (18 cm) above a shower curtain rod, shower door, or window treatment, so the undertreatment does not show in the swooped areas of the swag.

MATERIALS

- ◆ Decorator fabric.
- ◆ Curtain rod, 2½" (6.5 cm) wide. For shower opening, use spring-tension rod; for a window treatment, use a wall-mounted rod with a projection deep enough to clear undertreatment.
- ◆ Decorative buttons.
- ◆ Small, flat buttons, for reinforcement on the wrong side.

CUTTING DIRECTIONS

For the rod sleeve, cut a fabric strip 7 1/2" (19.3 cm) wide, piecing the strip as necessary to measure two-and-one-half to three times the length of the curtain rod. If using a wall-mount rod, the 7 1/2" (19.3 cm) fabric strip should be two-and-one-half to three times the combined length of the rod and the depth of the rod projection.

For the swag, cut a fabric rectangle, 33" (84 cm) wide, piecing it as necessary to measure one-and-one-half times the rod length plus 45" (115 cm); this allows for the swoops between the buttons and the draped fabric at the sides of the swag.

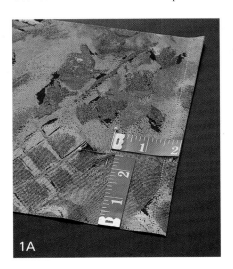

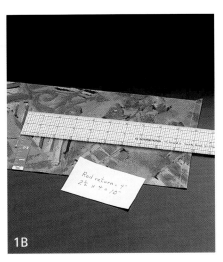

How to sew a buttoned swag

1A. FOR A SPRING-TENSION ROD. Press under 1/2" (1.3 cm) twice on the short ends of the fabric strip for the rod sleeve; stitch, to make 1/2" (1.3 cm) double-fold hems. Mark a point for the button placement at each end of fabric for the sleeve, measuring 2 1/2" (6.5 cm) from the lower edge and 2" (5 cm) from the hemmed edge.

1B. FOR A WALL-MOUNT ROD. Press under 1/2" (1.3 cm) twice on the short ends of the fabric strip for rod sleeve; stitch, to make 1/2" (1.3 cm) double-fold hems. Mark a point for the button placement at each end of the fabric for the sleeve, measuring 2 1/2" (6.5 cm) from the lower edge and measuring from each hemmed edge a distance equal to two-and-one-half times the depth of the rod projection.

Continued

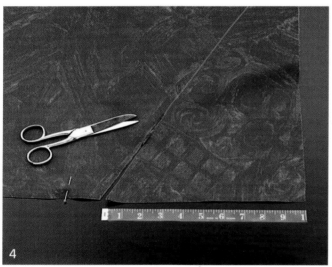

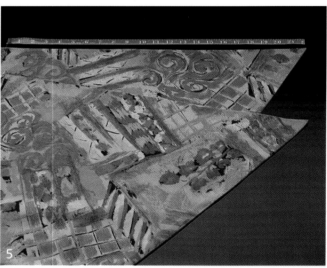

2. Divide the remaining length between the placement marks equally into desired number of swoops; mark placement for the buttons, 2½" (6.5 cm) up from the lower edge. Sew a button at each mark, positioning a reinforcement button on the wrong side of the fabric and a decorative button on the right side. Sew through both of the buttons at one time; form a thread shank under the decorative button if it does not have a shank.

3. Fold fabric strip for sleeve in half, right sides together. Stitch ½" (1.3 cm) seam on the long edge; press seam open. Turn the sleeve right side out, centering seam on back of sleeve. Buttons will be at or near lower edge.

4. Fold fabric for swag in half lengthwise, right sides together, with fold at top; pin long raw edges together at bottom. On the lower edge of swag, measure 10" (25.5 cm) from ends; mark. At each end, draw a line

from mark on lower edge to end of fold at top; cut away triangular section. Sew ½" (1.3 cm) seam around the ends and lower edge of swag, leaving an opening for turning on one short end; trim corners.

5. Turn swag right side out; press. Stitch the opening closed. On fold, measure 22" (56 cm) from each end of swag; mark the placement for vertical buttonholes, with upper end of buttonhole ½" (1.3 cm) from the fold.

6. Divide the remaining length between the marks equally into the desired number of swoops; mark buttonholes. At all placement marks on the swag, sew buttonholes large enough to accommodate the decorative buttons.

7. Measure a 2″ (5 cm) distance below each buttonhole; fold in half as shown, making 1″ (2.5 cm) tuck. Secure the tucks by hand-stitching them in place, or use machine bar tacks.

How to hang a buttoned swag

SPRING-TENSION ROD. Slide sleeve onto spring-tension rod, with the seam centered on back of rod and the buttons at or near lower edge. Mount rod at desired height. Distribute fullness evenly so the spaces between the buttons are equal. Button the swag onto shirred sleeve. Arrange the swoops between the buttons, draping the fabric as desired. Arrange the fabric at each end of the swag.

WALL-MOUNT ROD. Mount brackets on wall at desired location. Slide the sleeve onto curtain rod, with the seam centered on back of rod and buttons about ¼″ (6 mm) from the lower edge. Mount the curtain rod. Slide ends of sleeve onto the brackets; arrange the shirred sleeve so first and last buttons are located ½″ (1.3 cm) from corners on face of the rod. Hang and arrange the swag as for spring-tension rod.

Index

A

Accessories, decorative hardware, 9

Anchors, plastic, to install hardware, 9-10

B

Bishop sleeves, 25

Boards, mounting,

    covering, 11-12

    installing, 11-13

Butterfly swags, 47-49

Buttoned swags, 58-61

C

Combination seam, 16

Curtain rods, selecting, 8

Cutting and seaming fabric, 16-17

D

Double curtain rods, 8

Double rod-pocket swag, sewing, 55

Draping a swag, 24

E

Easy swags, 21-25

    scarf, 27-35

    shirred, 39-43

    variations, 36-37

F

Fabric, cutting and seaming, 16-17

Floor-puddled jabots, 25

French seam, 16

H

Hanging a buttoned swag, 61

Hardware, selecting and installing, 8-10

Heading, 14

Holdbacks, 9

I

Ideas for rod-pocket swags, 56-57

Inside-mounted board, installing, 11-12

Installing hardware, 9-10

J

Jabots, floor-puddled, 25

K

Knots, 37

L

Lined swags, 21, 23

M

Matching patterned fabrics, 17

Measuring, 14-15

Molly bolts, to install hardware, 10

Mounting boards,

    covering, 11-12

    installing, 11-13

Multiple swoops on scarf swags, 33-34

N

Nontraditional swags,

    butterfly, 47-49

    buttoned, 58-61

    rod-pocket, 50-57

O

Outside-mounted board, installing, 11, 13

P

Patterned fabrics, matching, 17

Plastic anchors, to install hardware, 9-10

Pole sets, 8, 37

Poufs on scarf swags, 27, 35

Projection, 14

R

Return, 14

Rod pocket, 14

Rod-pocket swags, 50-57

    double, 55

    single, 52-54, 56

    triple, 57

Rods, curtain, selecting, 8

S

Scarf swags, 27-35

    multiple swoops, 33-34

    poufs, 27, 35

    single swoops, 29-31

Seaming fabric, 16-17

Seams, types of, 16

Selecting and installing hardware, 8-10

Sewing swags,

    butterfly, 48-49

    buttoned, 59-61

    double rod-pocket, 55

    single rod-pocket, 52-54

Shelf brackets, as hardware, 37

Shirred swags, 39-43

Single rod-pocket swag, sewing, 52-54

Single swoops on scarf swags, 29-31

Straight-stitch seam, 16

Swag holders, 9, 27

Swag variations, 36-37

Swoops on scarf swags,

    multiple, 33-34

    single, 29-31

T

Tie-back holder, 9

Toggle anchors, plastic, to install hardware, 10

Towel rings, as hardware, 37

Triple rod-pocket swag, 57

U

Unlined swags, 21-23

V

Variations, swag, 36-37

Z

Zigzag seam, 16

5/98 Davidson 8.98

CY DECOSSE INCORPORATED

President/COO: Nino Tarantino
Executive V.P./Editor-in-Chief: William B. Jones
Chairman Emeritus: Cy DeCosse

Creative Touches™
Group Executive Editor: Zoe A. Graul
Managing Editor: Elaine Johnson
Editor: Linda Neubauer
Associate Creative Director: Lisa Rosenthal
Senior Art Director: Delores Swanson
Art Director: Mark Jacobson
Copy Editor: Janice Cauley
Desktop Publishing Specialist: Laurie Kristensen
Sample Production Manager: Carol Olson
Photo Studio Services Manager: Marcia Chambers
Publishing Production Manager: Kim Gerber

COWLES
Enthusiast Media

President/COO: Philip L. Penny

SWAGS ETC.
Created by: The Editors of Cy DeCosse Incorporated

Also available in the Creative Touches™ series:

*Stenciling Etc., Sponging Etc., Stone Finishes Etc., Valances Etc.,
Painted Designs Etc., Metallic Finishes Etc., Papering Projects Etc.*

The Creative Touches™ series draws from the individual titles of
The Home Decorating Institute®. Individual titles are also available
from the publisher and in bookstores and fabric stores.

Printed on American paper by:
R. R. Donnelley & Sons Co.
99 98 97 96 / 5 4 3 2 1

Cy DeCosse Incorporated offers a variety of how-to books.

For information write:
Cy DeCosse Subscriber Books
5900 Green Oak Drive
Minnetonka, MN 55343